Worry Less, Live More: A Practical Handbook for Overcoming Anxiety

By
Trevor Johnson

Introduction

Are you tired of being trapped in the tangled web of worry?

Introducing 'Worry Less, Live More: A Practical Handbook for Overcoming Anxiety.'

This empowering guide is designed to help you break free from the grips of anxiety and reclaim your life.

Packed with practical strategies and proven techniques, this handbook will equip you with the tools you need to conquer your fears and embrace a life of calm and contentment.

From understanding the root causes of anxiety to cultivating mindfulness and challenging negative thought patterns, each chapter offers actionable steps to help you navigate the ups and downs of life with confidence.

Say goodbye to anxiety and hello to a life filled with peace and joy.

Understanding Anxiety: Causes and Effects

Understanding anxiety requires identifying its underlying causes and recognizing the effects it has on your daily life. It's important to understand that anxiety doesn't just happen for no reason. There are specific causes and triggers that can contribute to its development.

These causes can vary from person to person, but common ones include a family history of anxiety, traumatic events, chronic medical conditions, and certain medications. Triggers, on the other hand, are specific situations or events that can make your anxiety worse. It could be something as simple as public speaking or as complex as a relationship issue.

By identifying these causes and triggers, you can start to gain a deeper understanding of your anxiety and take steps towards managing it more effectively.

The effects of anxiety can be far-reaching and have a significant impact on your daily life. In the short term, anxiety can cause physical symptoms such as rapid heartbeat, shortness of breath, and muscle tension. It can also lead to cognitive effects like racing thoughts, difficulty concentrating, and excessive worrying. These symptoms can make it challenging to perform everyday tasks and can interfere with your personal and professional life.

In the long term, untreated anxiety can have even more severe consequences. It can lead to the development of other mental health conditions, such as depression or substance abuse. It can also increase the risk of developing chronic physical health problems like heart disease or gastrointestinal issues.

Understanding the causes and effects of anxiety is an essential step in managing and overcoming it. With this knowledge, you can take proactive measures to reduce your anxiety and improve your overall well-being. Remember, you're not alone in this journey, and there's support available to help you navigate through it.

Recognizing the Signs of Anxiety

To effectively manage and overcome anxiety, it's crucial to be able to recognize the signs and symptoms that indicate its presence in your life. Anxiety can manifest in various ways, and being able to identify these signs will empower you to take proactive steps towards managing your anxiety and living a more fulfilling life.

Recognizing triggers is an essential aspect of understanding and managing anxiety. Triggers are situations, thoughts, or events that can cause an increase in anxiety levels. These triggers can vary from person to person, but some common examples include public speaking, crowded places, or even certain social situations. By identifying your triggers, you can better prepare yourself for potential anxiety-inducing situations and develop coping strategies to manage them effectively.

Coping strategies play a vital role in managing anxiety. When you recognize the signs of anxiety, it's important to have a toolbox of coping strategies at your disposal. These strategies can include deep breathing exercises, mindfulness techniques, physical activity, journaling, or seeking support from loved ones. Experiment with different strategies to find what works best for you and incorporate them into your daily routine. Remember, it's okay to ask for help or seek professional guidance if needed.

Recognizing the signs of anxiety is the first step towards effectively managing it. By identifying triggers and implementing coping strategies, you can regain control over your life and reduce the impact anxiety has on your overall well-being. Remember, you aren't alone in this journey, and with the right support and resources, you can overcome anxiety and live a life filled with peace and joy.

The Power of Mindfulness and Meditation

By incorporating mindfulness and meditation into your daily routine, you can further enhance your ability to manage and overcome anxiety. Mindfulness practices and meditation have been proven to be effective stress reduction techniques, allowing you to cultivate a greater sense of calm and peace in your life.

Mindfulness is the practice of bringing your attention to the present moment, without judgment. It involves focusing on your breath, sensations in your body, and the thoughts and emotions that arise, observing them without getting caught up in them. By cultivating this awareness, you can develop a greater understanding of your anxiety triggers and patterns.

Meditation, on the other hand, refers to the act of training your mind to focus and redirect your thoughts. It can involve various techniques, such as focusing on a specific object or repeating a mantra. By regularly practicing meditation, you can strengthen your ability to stay present and reduce anxiety.

Incorporating mindfulness and meditation into your daily routine doesn't have to be time-consuming or complicated. You can start with just a few minutes each day, gradually increasing the duration as you become more comfortable. Find a quiet and comfortable space where you can sit or lie down, and allow yourself to fully relax and let go.

As you engage in these practices, you may notice that your mind starts to wander or that anxious thoughts arise. This is normal. The key is to gently bring your attention back to the present moment, without judgment or frustration. Over time, you'll develop greater mental clarity and resilience, enabling you to better manage and overcome anxiety.

Here's a mindfulness script designed to help reduce worry and promote a sense of calm and presence:

Find a comfortable and quiet space. Sit or lie down, allowing your body to settle. Close your eyes gently, and take a few deep breaths. Inhale slowly through your nose, exhale gently through your mouth. Let each breath anchor you to the present moment.

1. Acknowledging Worry: *"Begin by acknowledging any worry or anxiety present. Accept these thoughts without judgment, recognizing that it's natural to experience concerns from time to time."*

2. Grounding Breath: *"Focus your attention on your breath. Feel the rise and fall of your chest with each inhale and exhale. Allow the breath to ground you in the present, gently guiding your awareness away from worry."*

3. Body Scan: *"Shift your focus to your body. Start from your toes and gradually move your attention upward. Notice any areas of tension or discomfort. With each exhale, release tension, allowing your body to soften and relax."*

4. Mindful Observation: *"Open your awareness to your surroundings. Notice the colors, shapes, and textures in the space around you. Engage your senses fully, bringing your attention to the present moment."*

5. Present-Moment Anchoring: *"Choose an anchor in the present moment. It could be the sensation of your breath, the warmth of your hands, or the sounds in your environment. Whenever worry surfaces, gently redirect your focus to this anchor."*

6. Labeling Thoughts: *"As worrisome thoughts arise, label them with neutral terms. For example, 'This is a worry about the future' or 'This is a concern about the past.' This labeling helps create distance from the thoughts."*

7. Breath Counting: *"Engage in breath counting to further calm the mind. Inhale deeply, counting 'one,' exhale, counting 'two.' Continue until you reach ten, then start again. If your mind wanders, gently bring it back to the counting."*

8. Gratitude Reflection: *"Shift your focus to gratitude. Reflect on three things you are grateful for in this* *moment. Gratitude redirects your mind toward positive aspects of life, diminishing the hold of worry."*

9. Loving-Kindness Meditation: *"Extend feelings of love and kindness to yourself. Silently repeat phrases like 'May I be happy, may I be healthy, may I be at peace.' Allow these intentions to create a sense of warmth and comfort."*

10. Closing Reflection: *"Take a moment to notice how you feel now compared to the beginning. Embrace the sense of calm and presence you've cultivated. Know that you have the power to return to this state whenever needed."*

When you're ready, gently open your eyes. Carry this sense of mindfulness with you, using these techniques whenever worry arises. You are the architect of your mental landscape, capable of cultivating peace and tranquility.

Breathing Techniques for Instant Calm

To achieve instant calm, practice simple breathing techniques to help ease anxiety. Deep breathing exercises and relaxation techniques can be powerful tools in reducing stress and promoting a sense of calmness. Here are four techniques you can try anytime, anywhere:

- **Diaphragmatic Breathing:** Sit or lie down comfortably and place one hand on your chest and the other on your abdomen. Take a slow, deep breath in through your nose, feeling your abdomen rise as you fill your lungs with air. Exhale slowly through your mouth, feeling your abdomen fall. Focus on the sensation of your breath and repeat for several minutes.
- **4-7-8 Breathing:** Close your eyes and take a deep breath in through your nose for a count of four. Hold your breath for a count of seven. Exhale slowly through your mouth for a count of eight. Repeat this cycle four times. This technique helps regulate your breath and activate the body's relaxation response.
- **Box Breathing:** Visualize a box and imagine tracing its four sides with your breath. Inhale deeply for a count of four as you trace the first side, hold your breath for a count of four as you trace the second side, exhale for a count of four as you trace the third side, and hold your breath

again for a count of four as you trace the fourth side. Repeat this pattern for several rounds.

- **Breath Counting:** Close your eyes and take a deep breath in. As you exhale, silently count 'one.' Inhale deeply again and exhale, counting 'two.' Continue counting your breaths up to ten, then start again from one. If you lose count, simply return to one and begin again. This technique helps focus your mind and bring a sense of calm.

Challenging Negative Thought Patterns

Challenge each negative thought that arises in your mind by questioning its validity and replacing it with a more positive and realistic perspective. Challenging negative thought patterns is an important step in overcoming anxiety and regaining control over your thoughts and emotions. Cognitive restructuring techniques can help you identify and challenge irrational thoughts, allowing you to replace them with more accurate and positive ones.

One effective technique is called 'thought stopping.' When a negative thought arises, imagine a big red stop sign in your mind. Say 'stop' to yourself and redirect your attention to something positive or calming. This interrupts the negative thought pattern and helps you regain control.

Another technique is called 'thought challenging.' Start by identifying the negative thought and ask yourself if there's any evidence to support it. Often, negative thoughts are based on assumptions or past experiences that may not be relevant to the present situation. Replace the negative thought with a more realistic and positive one. For example, if you catch yourself thinking 'I'm not good enough,' challenge this thought by reminding yourself of past successes and acknowledging your strengths and abilities.

Practicing self-compassion is also crucial in challenging negative thought patterns. Treat yourself with kindness and understanding, just as you'd a close friend. Acknowledge that everyone makes mistakes and that it's okay to have negative thoughts. Instead of judging yourself harshly, offer yourself words of encouragement and support.

Incorporating these cognitive restructuring techniques and self-compassion practices into your daily life can help you challenge and replace negative thought patterns, leading to a more positive and realistic perspective. Remember, it takes time and practice, so be patient with yourself. You have the power to change your thoughts and live a more fulfilling and anxiety-free life.

Building a Support Network: Friends and Family

Surround yourself with a reliable network of friends and family who can offer support and understanding during times of anxiety. Building a support network is an essential part of managing anxiety and finding a sense of comfort and security.

Here are four ways to build a strong support network:

- **Building a support network: professional help**: Seeking professional help can be a valuable addition to your support network. Therapists and counselors are trained to provide guidance and support, offering strategies to cope with anxiety. They can help you develop healthy coping mechanisms and provide a safe space for you to express your feelings and concerns.
- **Building a support network: online communities**: Online communities can provide a sense of belonging and understanding. Joining support groups or forums specifically dedicated to anxiety can connect you with individuals who are going through similar experiences. These communities offer a platform to share your thoughts, gain valuable insights, and receive support from people who truly understand what you're going through.
- **Lean on friends and family**: Surrounding yourself with loved ones who genuinely care

about your well-being can make a world of difference. Reach out to friends or family members who are empathetic and understanding. Share your struggles, and let them know how they can support you. Sometimes, all it takes is a listening ear or a comforting presence to help alleviate anxiety.

- **Communicate your needs**: Building a support network requires effective communication. Be open and honest about your anxiety with your loved ones. Let them know what triggers your anxiety and how they can help support you. By expressing your needs, you empower those around you to provide the support you require.

Therapy Options: Finding the Right Fit

Finding the right therapy option for you is crucial in effectively managing and overcoming anxiety. It's understandable that the idea of seeking therapy can feel overwhelming, but remember that you're taking a positive step towards improving your mental health. There are various therapy options available, and finding the right fit may require some exploration and trial.

When it comes to finding the right therapist, it's important to consider your specific needs and preferences. Start by asking for recommendations from trusted friends, family, or healthcare professionals. They may be able to suggest therapists who specialize in anxiety or have had success in treating similar cases. Additionally, you can conduct online research to find therapists in your area who've experience in anxiety disorders.

Online therapy options have become increasingly popular and convenient. They offer flexibility in terms of scheduling and allow you to receive therapy from the comfort of your own home. Many online platforms have a wide range of therapists to choose from, so you can find someone who suits your needs and preferences. It's important to ensure that the online therapy platform you choose is reputable and employs licensed therapists.

Remember that therapy is a collaborative process, and finding the right therapist is essential for building a strong therapeutic relationship. Take the time to schedule a consultation or an initial session with potential therapists to assess their approach and determine if you feel comfortable working with them.

Ultimately, finding the right therapy option is a personal decision. Trust your instincts and don't hesitate to explore different options until you find the right fit. Remember, therapy is a valuable tool in managing anxiety, and with the right therapist, you can make significant progress towards living a more fulfilling and anxiety-free life.

Taking Control of Your Physical Health

To effectively manage and overcome anxiety, prioritize taking control of your physical health by incorporating regular exercise and healthy lifestyle habits. When it comes to anxiety, physical activity and nutrition play a crucial role in promoting overall well-being and reducing stress levels. Here are four key ways to take control of your physical health and support your journey towards a more balanced and anxiety-free life:

- **Engage in regular physical activity:** Physical activity has been shown to release endorphins, which are natural mood-boosting chemicals in the brain. Incorporating regular exercise into your routine can help reduce anxiety symptoms and improve your overall mental health. Whether it's going for a brisk walk, attending a fitness class, or practicing yoga, find an activity that you enjoy and make it a priority in your schedule.
- **Eat a balanced diet:** Proper nutrition is essential for maintaining good physical and mental health. Avoid skipping meals or relying on processed foods, as they can contribute to feelings of fatigue and worsen anxiety symptoms. Instead, focus on consuming a well-rounded diet that includes plenty of fruits, vegetables, whole grains, and lean proteins. These nutrient-rich foods provide the energy and nourishment your body needs to function optimally.

- **Get enough sleep:** A lack of sleep can significantly impact your mental health and increase anxiety levels. Aim for 7-9 hours of quality sleep each night to ensure your body has enough time to rest and recharge. Establish a bedtime routine and create a sleep-friendly environment to promote relaxation and better sleep.
- **Practice stress management techniques:** In addition to physical activity and nutrition, incorporating stress management techniques into your daily routine can help alleviate anxiety. Consider practices such as deep breathing exercises, meditation, journaling, or engaging in hobbies that bring you joy and relaxation. These activities can help reduce stress and promote a sense of calmness in your daily life.

Embracing a Healthy Lifestyle: Diet and Exercise

Prioritize your physical well-being by incorporating a balanced diet and regular exercise into your daily routine to embrace a healthy lifestyle. When it comes to anxiety, taking care of your body is just as important as taking care of your mind. Healthy eating and fitness routines can have a significant impact on reducing anxiety levels and improving overall well-being.

Let's start with healthy eating. A nutritious diet rich in fruits, vegetables, whole grains, lean proteins, and healthy fats can provide your body with the essential nutrients it needs to function optimally. Certain foods, like those high in omega-3 fatty acids, can even help reduce inflammation in the brain, which is linked to anxiety. By fueling your body with the right nutrients, you can boost your mood and energy levels, making it easier to manage stress and anxiety.

In addition to a healthy diet, incorporating regular exercise into your daily routine is crucial. Exercise releases endorphins, which are natural mood boosters and stress relievers. Engaging in physical activity, whether it's going for a run, attending a yoga class, or even taking a brisk walk, can help you release tension and clear your mind. Not only does exercise improve your physical health, but it also has a positive impact on your mental well-being, helping to reduce anxiety and improve overall mood.

Remember, embracing a healthy lifestyle is a journey, and it's important to be patient and kind to yourself along the way. Start small by making simple changes to your diet and incorporating short bursts of physical activity into your day. Over time, you'll notice the positive effects on both your physical and mental health.

The Role of Sleep in Managing Anxiety

Getting enough sleep is essential for managing anxiety and promoting overall well-being. When you don't get enough sleep, it can significantly impact your mental health and increase anxiety levels.

Here are four important points to consider when it comes to the role of sleep in managing anxiety:

- **The importance of relaxation techniques:** Incorporating relaxation techniques into your bedtime routine can help calm your mind and prepare your body for sleep. Deep breathing exercises, progressive muscle relaxation, and meditation can all be effective ways to promote relaxation and reduce anxiety before bed.
- **The impact of caffeine on anxiety levels:** Consuming caffeine, especially close to bedtime, can interfere with your ability to fall asleep and stay asleep. It's important to limit or avoid caffeine intake, especially if you struggle with anxiety. Opt for decaffeinated beverages or herbal teas instead.
- **Establishing a consistent sleep schedule:** Going to bed and waking up at the same time every day helps regulate your body's internal clock and promotes better sleep. Create a bedtime routine that includes relaxing activities and stick to it as much as possible, even on weekends.

- **Creating a sleep-friendly environment:** Make your bedroom a peaceful and comfortable space that promotes relaxation. Keep the room cool, dark, and quiet. Consider using blackout curtains, earplugs, or white noise machines to block out any external disturbances that could disrupt your sleep.

Effective Time Management for Reduced Stress

By effectively managing your time, you can reduce stress and create a sense of control in your daily life. Time management is a skill that can greatly impact your overall well-being and productivity.

One effective technique to implement is time blocking. This involves dividing your day into specific blocks of time dedicated to different tasks or activities. By allocating time for specific activities, you can ensure that you have enough time to complete all your tasks and avoid feeling overwhelmed.

Prioritizing tasks is another crucial aspect of effective time management. Start by identifying which tasks are most important and need to be completed first. This can help you focus your time and energy on the tasks that truly matter. It's also important to set realistic goals and expectations for yourself. Remember that you're only human and can't do everything at once. By setting achievable goals, you can avoid feeling overwhelmed and reduce unnecessary stress.

Another helpful tip is to minimize distractions during your designated work time. Turn off notifications on your phone or computer, and find a quiet and comfortable workspace. This can help you stay focused and be more productive. Additionally, take regular breaks to recharge and refresh your mind. This can actually improve your overall productivity and prevent burnout.

Effective time management requires consistency and discipline. It may take some time to find a routine that works best for you, but with practice, it will become second nature. Remember to be flexible and adapt your schedule when unexpected events arise.

Setting Realistic Goals and Priorities

To effectively manage your time and reduce stress, it's important to set realistic goals and priorities. Realistic goal setting allows you to establish clear objectives that are attainable and within your reach. It helps you avoid the overwhelming feeling of constantly falling short of your expectations. By setting realistic goals, you set yourself up for success and build confidence in your ability to accomplish what you set out to do.

Here are four tips to help you with realistic goal setting and prioritizing tasks:

- **Start with small, achievable goals:** Break down your larger goals into smaller, more manageable tasks. This not only makes them less overwhelming but also allows you to celebrate small victories along the way. By focusing on achievable tasks, you build momentum and maintain motivation.
- **Prioritize tasks based on importance and urgency:** Not all tasks are created equal. It's essential to identify which tasks are the most important and need to be done immediately. By prioritizing tasks, you ensure that you're allocating your time and energy to the things that matter most.
- **Be flexible and adaptable:** Life is unpredictable, and things don't always go as planned. It's

important to be flexible and willing to adjust your goals and priorities when necessary. Embrace change and see it as an opportunity for growth rather than a setback.

- **Set realistic timelines:** Give yourself enough time to complete tasks without feeling rushed or overwhelmed. Be mindful of your limitations and consider any external factors that may impact your timeline. Setting realistic timelines allows you to work at a steady pace and reduces the chances of feeling stressed or burnt out.

Cultivating Positive Relationships and Boundaries

Cultivating positive relationships and setting healthy boundaries is crucial for managing anxiety and promoting overall well-being. When it comes to anxiety, having strong connections with others can provide a sense of support, understanding, and comfort. Nurturing meaningful connections allows you to share your thoughts and feelings, knowing that you aren't alone in your struggles. These relationships can offer a safe space to express yourself, seek advice, and receive encouragement.

However, it's equally important to cultivate healthy boundaries within these relationships. Boundaries act as a protective shield, preventing others from crossing lines that may cause stress or discomfort. By setting clear boundaries, you can create a sense of control and ensure that your emotional needs are met. It's okay to say 'no' when you need to, and it's crucial to communicate your boundaries openly and honestly.

To cultivate healthy boundaries, start by identifying your limits and values. Reflect on what makes you feel comfortable and what makes you feel overwhelmed or anxious. Communicate these boundaries to others, letting them know what's acceptable and what's not. Remember, setting boundaries isn't about being selfish, but rather about prioritizing your well-being.

Nurturing meaningful connections and cultivating healthy boundaries go hand in hand. By surrounding yourself with supportive and understanding individuals, you can create a network of people who uplift and empower you. Together, you can navigate through life's challenges and celebrate its joys. So, take the time to invest in your relationships and set boundaries that align with your needs. You deserve to have positive connections that contribute to your overall well-being and help you manage anxiety.

Overcoming Procrastination and Perfectionism

Overcoming procrastination and perfectionism requires recognizing the detrimental impact they can have on your mental well-being and taking proactive steps to address them. It's important to understand that these tendencies can often stem from self-doubt and a fear of not meeting expectations. However, by implementing the following strategies, you can begin to overcome these challenges and live a more fulfilling life:

- **Break tasks into smaller, manageable steps:** When faced with a daunting task, it's easy to become overwhelmed and put it off. By breaking it down into smaller, more achievable steps, you can make progress without feeling overwhelmed. This not only helps you overcome procrastination but also allows you to build confidence along the way.
- **Challenge perfectionistic thinking:** Perfectionism can be paralyzing, as it sets unrealistically high standards that are impossible to meet. Instead of striving for perfection, aim for excellence and progress. Recognize that mistakes are a part of growth and learning, and embrace the process rather than fixating on the outcome.
- **Set realistic goals and timelines:** Managing expectations is crucial in overcoming procrastination and perfectionism. Set realistic goals that are achievable within a given

timeframe. This will help you stay focused and motivated without succumbing to the pressure of perfection.

- **Practice self-compassion:** Be kind to yourself and understand that nobody is perfect. When faced with self-doubt, remind yourself of your strengths and accomplishments. Treat yourself with the same kindness and understanding that you'd offer a friend facing similar challenges.

Celebrating Progress: Embracing a Life of Freedom From Anxiety

When you prioritize celebrating your progress, you can truly embrace a life of freedom from anxiety. It's important to acknowledge and appreciate the steps you have taken towards overcoming anxiety. Embracing gratitude for your journey can bring a sense of fulfillment and propel you forward on your path to finding inner peace.

Take a moment to reflect on how far you have come. Recognize the small victories along the way, whether it's facing a fear, implementing coping strategies, or seeking support. Each step forward, no matter how small, is a testament to your strength and resilience. By celebrating these milestones, you reinforce positive behaviors and build confidence in your ability to overcome anxiety.

Gratitude plays a significant role in cultivating a mindset of abundance and contentment. It shifts your focus from what's lacking to what you have accomplished. Embrace gratitude by keeping a journal and writing down three things you're grateful for each day. This practice can help you shift your perspective, allowing you to see the progress you have made and the positive aspects of your life.

Finding inner peace is a journey, and it requires embracing the present moment and letting go of worries about the future or regrets from the past. Celebrating progress allows you to be present and fully engage in the process of overcoming anxiety. It reminds you that anxiety doesn't define you, and that you're capable of living a fulfilling and anxiety-free life.

Frequently Asked Questions

How Can I Overcome Procrastination and Perfectionism?

To overcome procrastination and perfectionism, it's important to recognize that self-doubt often fuels these behaviors.

Start by setting realistic goals and breaking tasks into smaller, manageable steps.

Practice self-compassion and remind yourself that mistakes are a natural part of learning and growth.

Building self-confidence is key, so celebrate your accomplishments, big or small.

Remember, it's about progress, not perfection.

With time and practice, you can overcome these obstacles and find a healthier, happier balance.

What Are Some Effective Time Management Techniques for Reducing Stress?

To reduce stress and manage your time effectively, try implementing some effective strategies.

Start by prioritizing your tasks based on their importance and deadlines.

Break down larger tasks into smaller, more manageable ones to avoid feeling overwhelmed.

Use a planner or digital calendar to schedule your activities and set reminders.

Take regular breaks to avoid burnout and maintain productivity.

How Can I Cultivate Positive Relationships and Set Boundaries?

Cultivating healthy relationships and setting personal boundaries are essential for your overall well-being. By actively investing in positive relationships, you can create a support system that uplifts and empowers you.

It's important to surround yourself with people who respect your boundaries and understand your needs. Communicate openly and honestly with others about your limits and expectations.

What Are Some Therapy Options for Managing Anxiety?

When it comes to managing anxiety, there are a few therapy options that may be helpful.

One option is Cognitive Behavioral Therapy (CBT), which focuses on identifying and changing negative thought patterns and behaviors. CBT can provide you with tools and strategies to better cope with anxiety.

Another option is medication, which can be prescribed by a doctor to help manage symptoms.

It's important to discuss these options with a mental health professional to determine what approach is best for you.

How Can I Celebrate My Progress and Embrace a Life Free From Anxiety?

You can celebrate your progress and embrace a life free from anxiety by embracing mindfulness and finding gratitude.

Taking the time to be present and fully engage in the present moment can help you let go of worries and fears.

Practicing gratitude can shift your focus towards the positive aspects of your life, fostering a sense of contentment and peace.

Conclusion

Congratulations on completing 'Worry Less, Live More: A Practical Handbook for Overcoming Anxiety!' By learning powerful mindfulness techniques, challenging negative thought patterns, and setting realistic goals, you have taken the first step towards a life free from anxiety.

Imagine this: Sarah, a young professional, struggled with anxiety her whole life. But through the practices in this handbook, she finally found peace and confidence, allowing her to excel in her career and form fulfilling relationships.

Embrace the tools in this book and create your own success story. You deserve a life of freedom from anxiety.

The information provided in this book, "Worry Less, Live More: A Practical Handbook for Overcoming Anxiety," is intended for general informational purposes only. The content is not a substitute for professional advice or treatment.

The author and publisher of this book are not licensed mental health professionals, and the content does not constitute psychological, medical, or therapeutic advice. Readers are encouraged to seek the guidance of qualified professionals for personalized advice regarding their individual circumstances.

Made in United States
Troutdale, OR
02/05/2024

17449808R00022